D1490646

Thinking
Statistically

URI BRAM

Copyright © 2012 Uri Bram

Look, the Berne Convention means that copyright accrues to authors automatically in almost-all jurisdictions – legal boilerplate at the bottom of a page doesn't really have anything to do with it. What's more, both of us know that it's pretty unlikely I'll be able to do much if you do decide to copy this book. So let's just say that I worked quite hard on it and would appreciate if you didn't copy. Thanks very much, and hope you enjoy it.

All rights reserved.

ISBN: 1469912333
ISBN-13: 978-1469912332

To ELIZABETH SWERDLOW,
MY FAVOURITE STATISTICIAN

TABLE OF CONTENTS

INTRODUCTION

You're smart. Really smart. People are always complimenting your curiosity and your general knack for understanding things; maybe you even have a diploma from a fancy university, though that's irrelevant for our purposes. You're really smart, but (deep breath) you don't understand Bayes' Theorem. Or endogeneity. Or selection bias. Maybe you've never heard of them, maybe you read about them once in a textbook. You definitely don't use them in your everyday life. It's not your fault: for reasons completely beyond me, rarely does anyone explain these concepts to you properly unless you happen to be studying statistical techniques. But Bayes and selection bias and endogeneity are concepts, not techniques; understanding them is essentially independent from knowing how to find a p-value, or the conditions for using a Student's t-distribution, or the proof of the Central Limit Theorem.

Concepts and abstractions are often useful even if you aren't exactly interested in the details underneath them. It's good to understand that if the Central Bank raises interest rates then people tend to save more, without understanding the technical details of how a Central Bank effects interest rate changes. It's good to understand that there are sets of chords that harmonise together, and that many pop-songs are based on a few simple progressions, without understanding anything deeper about music (or physics). It's good to understand the logic of evolutionary theory, even if you never plan to dust a fossil or examine mitochondrial D.N.A. Similarly, there's actually no good reason why you have to learn statistical techniques in order to understand statistical concepts, and the concepts on their own can be a huge help when examining and interpreting the world around us.

Most statisticians (and econometricians, and scientists) use statistics informally in their everyday lives, and a surprising number assume that everyone else does too. The world is made up of information, and we make all kinds of decisions and judgments based on the information that reaches us: if that information is systematically biased or incomplete then the decisions we make will be systematically wrong. Formal statistics is about taking precise, detailed information and proving exactly what that information can or can't tell us; informal statistics is about taking the vague, general patterns of information that we see in everyday life and using the same basic statistical concepts to make generally better decisions and judgments. Not perfect judgments, sure, and not ones you can hang numbers on, but a better judgment is a better judgment and small improvements add up fast.

This book will teach you how to think like a statistician, without worrying about formal statistical techniques. Along the way we'll learn how selection bias can explain why your boss doesn't know he sucks (even when everyone else does); how to use Bayes' Theorem to decide if your partner is cheating on you; and why Mark Zuckerberg should never be used as an example for anything. At no point will we do anything involving numbers. You can handle numbers just fine, if you want to, but you don't right now.

This book is for you.

ALTERNATIVE USES

If I'm going to be honest here — and if you and I are going to do a book together then honesty is very important — I have a second hope for this book, and then a third.

The second hope is that the book can be useful for people taking traditional statistics courses, as a companion and refresher on the ideas behind the work they're doing. The truth is that nobody, no matter how statistically-minded they are, can consistently remember every idea they need to know and the key intuitions behind how things work. Don't ever forget it — these ideas aren't easy, and everyone has to look up the definitions sometimes. I hope that this book might provide a concise and accessible summary of some of the key concepts to people knee-deep in formal tests.

The third hope is that —well— Hal Varian, the chief economist of Google, has said that "the sexy job in the next 10 years will be statisticians... And I'm not kidding."[i] I hope this book will make everyone who reads it as sexy as a statistician. Although people who choose to read this book seem to be exceptionally sexy already, so it might be hard to tell cause from effect.

CHAPTER ONE:
SELECTION

BUYING PEACHES

So, it's Sunday morning (the birds in one another's arms, cats in the trees) and you're going to a market stall to buy some peaches. You pick up a couple; you poke them, shake them, and check them for blemishes. If they seem pretty good then you grab another twenty and put the whole lot in your shopping bag. You have just drawn an inference (that the peaches are good) about a whole population (all the peaches at this market stall) based on one small sample (the first few peaches).

Whether you like it or not, you have just performed something called "inferential statistics." If you were a more formal statistician you could run some fancy tests and figure out very precise things about the apple-population: for example, the probability that all the peaches at the stall are good, given that a certain number of randomly-selected samples were. But for any normal purposes, the first few peaches are a good-enough indicator of the quality of the rest.

They are only a reasonable indicator, though, if they are a (fairly) random selection from the population of peaches as a whole. This is probably true if you chose them yourself. But what if, instead, the stall-holder saw you gazing peachwards and proffered you two to poke at? Now you would have very little reason to trust that the sample-peaches were representative of the general population: if the stall-holder is wily, and if she doesn't expect to see you again, then it's plenty likely that she uses her best peaches as samples and so hides the fact that the rest are pretty bad. In statistics, this issue has the snazzy name of Selection Bias: basically, that your inferences will be biased if you use a non-random sample and pretend that it's random.

SELF-BIASING DATA

In the apple example, the source of bias is obvious — the stall-holder's nefariousness. If her trick succeeds it's because we aren't paying attention;

with a moment's pause, nobody would believe that the stall-holder's choice is even vaguely random. But often its much harder to tell a good (informal) sample from a bad one, partly because data samples can inadvertently bias themselves. There are lots of valid things we can say about a population from a smaller sample of it, if that sample is truly random. There are even lots of valid things we can say about a population if our sample is biased in some systematic way that we understand and correct for. The real problems occur when our sample is biased and we fail to account for that.

Imagine, for example, that you go to a daycare centre to take a survey of the children's ages. Your sample is the children who showed up that morning, and your population is all the children who ever attend that daycare. So far so good: some children will be missing today, but assuming it's a normal morning there's no reason to think that the missing-ness will relate to age. Then you shout for all the one-year-olds to please stand up and be counted, then the same for all the two-year-olds, and finally the three-year-olds. Any researcher would notice here that not all the children had stood. But a bad researcher would assume that the missing datapoints were missing at random, and could safely be ignored.

Now, any survey which can't absolutely coerce answers from every desired respondent will inevitably face some degree of non-responsiveness, and so long as the missing datapoints are genuinely missing-at-random it really is safe to ignore them. However, in our daycare example, there's a clear possibility that the data is missing dependent on the value it would have taken. Younger children are quite liable to be under-represented in our sample, since one-year-olds are less likely to understand our instructions, less likely to co-operate even when they do understand, and more likely to be distracted by a particularly interesting bug. Our sample is biased towards kids who've got their heads together.

THINKING GRAPHICALLY

One way to understand this kind of selection selection bias is to think of it visually. Imagine yourself attending a talk in a big auditorium. The speaker comes up to the microphone and taps it thrice, like she's seen people do in the movies. *Thump thump thump.* She fiddles with her hair and pulls the microphone up to her chin. "Can everyone hear me?," she asks. Suppose that, in actual fact, one-third of the audience can hear her perfectly; one-third can only *kinda* hear her; and one-third can't hear her at all. If we draw the entire audience as a big square, and divide it into three equal parts, we get this:

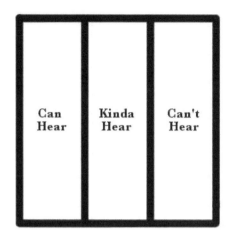

But will the responses she get reflect this even three-way split? Clearly not. Imagine (unrealistically) that this entire audience is incredibly keen to answer questions at public talks, and will try to participate whenever they can. As such, when she asks "Can everyone hear me?", all the people who can hear clearly will simultaneously answer "we can hear you!" (with great gusto). Among the people who can kinda hear her, half will answer "we kinda-hear you!", while the other half stay quiet because they didn't quite catch what happened. Among the people who can't hear, nobody will do anything because they won't realise the talk started (alright, I admit that in real life this would work entirely differently, but play along with the stylisation). If we shade The Responders in grey, the audience will look like this:

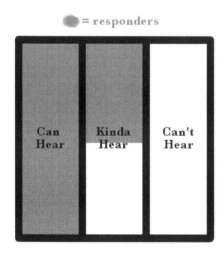

From the speaker's point of view, the only audience members who "exist" are the ones who responded to her question. She hasn't read any helpful statistical-thinking books, so she doesn't know about selection bias, and doesn't notice that the only audience members who can answer her question are the ones who (without even realising it) are 'selected' into her sample by hearing her question and then answering it. From her point of view, the audience looks like this:

To put that in perspective, let's place this sample within the outline of the original population:

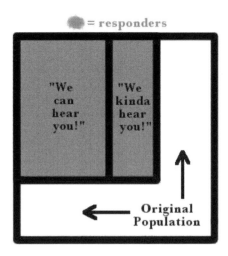

Now we can compare the speaker's conclusions about the audience with the objective truth. First, and most obviously, the speaker assumes that everyone in the audience can hear her at least partially. This is the selection bias problem, whereby the people who can't hear at all don't respond at all and are missing from the final sample. Second, the speaker is wrong about the balance of numbers even among the people who can hear her at least a little: she believes that two-thirds of the audience can hear her clearly, and only one-third are having any trouble, so her general impression is that she's roughly at the right volume. This is completely untrue, of course: in fact, there are equal numbers who can hear her clearly and who can hear her poorly, but the ones who can only just hear her are less likely to respond to her question and so are *partially* under-represented among respondents, while the people who can't hear her at all are *completely* unrepresented. Third, the speaker only receives data from half of the total relevant population, but either assumes that she *is* receiving data from the whole population or that the data she receives is from a random sample. Both of these assumptions are easy enough to make: we often don't really know what the total relevant population size for a particular question is, so it's easy to assume that the data we're receiving (more or less) represents all the data that exists; second, even when we know that some amount of non-response is happening, the effortless assumption is that it's probably random and doesn't make a difference. Probably the best way to stay vigilant against these kinds of mistakes is by being aware of the theoretical issues behind selection bias: if you're on the lookout they'll find it much harder to sneak past you.

GRAPHING THE ABSTRACT

In the previous example, the mechanism of the selection bias — how well people can hear the speaker — is easy to interpret in a graphical way: maybe the auditorium really *is* a big square, and maybe the speaker is standing on the left hand side of the square, and maybe the people who can hear her clearly *are* the ones sitting in the front third of the auditorium, and maybe the people who can't hear her *are* the ones sitting at the back. (You might even wonder if your humble author selected this example exactly because it had an obvious physical/graphical interpretation). However, there will also be situations where the graphic I presented only represents the audience's comprehension in a 'metaphorical' way: for example, maybe one-third of the audience can lipread (so they can understand the speaker perfectly even when they can't hear her), one-third of the audience is playing on their new Kindle Fires (so they only kinda-hear the speaker, no matter how clearly she speaks), and one-third of the audience doesn't actually speak English (so they can't "hear" her at all, no matter what). Maybe all these people are distributed randomly through the auditorium, and their seating position has no effect on how well they hear the speaker: the same three-part diagram is still a good visual representation of the *situation* we're dealing with, just that now we need to think of it as a metaphor rather than as a factual physical depiction of some kind.

Similarly, it's possible to think about any kind of selection bias problem in the same graphical manner, regardless of whether there's a meaningful real-world physical interpretation of the graphic: we just imagine the data occupying an imaginary metaphorical "space," and then shade out part of that space according to which information reaches the final sample. This way of thinking about selection bias either will or won't be appealing and useful for you: if it isn't, feel free to ignore it and skip to the next segment. These kinds of stats visualisations are not an "official" part of statistical thinking in any way, they're just part of a strategy for interpreting and internalising statistics concepts which could be helpful if it happens to click with you.

Let's look at an example where the graphic is *purely* metaphorical. A few short pages ago we were talking about a survey we took at a daycare centre, to determine the ages of the children there. We noted that the responses would be susceptible to selection bias, because the youngest children would be least likely to respond to the question. To give us something concrete to work with, let's say that *all* the three-year-olds respond; *two-thirds* of the two-year-olds respond; and *one-third* of the one-year-olds respond. Let's say that there are equal numbers of one, two and three year olds in the total population. Drawing that graphically we get something like this:

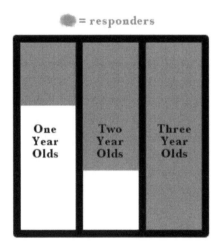

Once again, that's not some kind of physical 'space' that the kids are crowded into (good luck getting kindergartners to line up *anywhere*); it's a kind of imaginary "information space" that we're using to help us think about the problem.

Another way to graphically represent the same information is to re-arrange the layout such that all of the non-responders are clumped together:

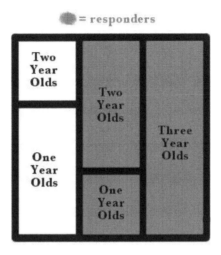

This representation shows clearly that two-thirds of the total population responded; that all the three-year-olds responded; that two-thirds of the two-year-olds responded (the grey two-year-olds block is twice the size of the white two-year-olds block); and that one-third of the one-year-olds responded (the grey one-year-olds block is half the size of the white one-year-olds block). It also shows that half the responders were three-year-olds (the grey three-year-olds block is half of all the grey in the graphic); one-third of the responders were two-year-olds; and one-sixth were one-year-olds (you could measure the graphic or just trust me on that one).

What if, for some reason, you're not overly fond of squares? You could also try representing the 'information space' as, say, pie charts:

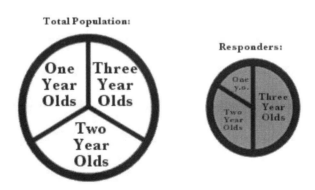

The pie charts are scaled relative to each other, so the responders' pie chart has two-thirds of the area of the total population pie chart because the responders were two-thirds of the total population. The first pie chart shows clearly that each age group makes up one-third of the total population; the second pie chart shows clearly that three-year-olds make up half the responder sample, two-year-olds make up two-thirds of the responder sample, and one-year-olds make up one-third of the responder sample. It doesn't show clearly the proportions within each group who responded: you'd have to be *very* good at eyeballing to figure out that e.g. one-third of the one-year-olds responded overall.

None of these representations is in any way sacrosanct: they're all just improvisations that I developed while thinking about the problem as selections from within a physical space. As should be clear by now, there's no real right way to graphically represent information: if you like playing with shapes in your head (or scribbling on paper), you could try thinking about selection bias problems graphically and seeing if that gets you anywhere. But this truly is an "optional exercise" intended only for those who find it helpful: at this point we'll move back to describing selection bias cases with words instead of pictures, but you're welcome to imagine the situations in visual forms wherever appropriate.

PRESIDENT TRUMAN AND THE CENSUS

You might be thinking that the examples of selection bias so far in this book have all been small-scale and silly, and you may be right. But they represent a deep and genuine problem with sample selection that plagues even professional statisticians. Perhaps the most notorious example of selection bias in public surveys is Democrat Harry Truman's "upset" election victory in the 1948 U.S. Presidential election, which every pollster had predicted he was going to lose by a landslide. Where did the pollsters go wrong? They had based their numbers on a series of telephone surveys — probably the most extensive, expensive and scientific telephone survey that had ever been done — and which confidently predicted a Republican victory. But who owned a telephone in 1948? Well, generally wealthier people. Who happened to lean Republican.[ii]

As another example, the U.S. Census Bureau has perpetual problems calculating the national population, despite a tremendous effort and the power of government behind them. And we're not talking a couple of missing people: after the 2000 Census, the Bureau estimated that 4.5 million people were missing from its count, largely low-income Blacks and Hispanics.[iii] For all kinds of reasons, the probability that a person will fail to return her census forms is related to her other attributes: her socioeconomic status, her family situation, her location, her education levels, perhaps her ethnicity. The people at the Census Bureau are fully aware of these issues, and make heroic efforts both to chase up non-responders and to publicise the shortcomings of their final counts. But the non-responses will inevitably occur, and occur in a strongly non-random way. This is not just an academic problem: the census numbers are supposed to determine the funds that local governments receive from the federal government for social services. If residents of low-income urban neighbourhoods are unusually likely to go missing from the census, low-income urban neighbourhoods will receive less funds than they truly deserve.

THE FEEDBACK EFFECT

It's safe to assume that you weren't planning to run a major presidential poll or national census in the next few weeks, but similar effects haunt our everyday lives. For example, "feedback systems" in schools, companies, charities, and governments often suffer because the probability of a subordinate's opinion actually reaching the authorities is strongly related to whether the person's opinion was positive or negative. Bosses, donors, and academic deans often have impressions about their organisation that seem utterly wacky to their less-pleased subordinates. But when the bosses' knowledge is based on the feedback that has been volunteered to them, and if they fail to correct for the bias in this sample, it's little wonder that they reach incorrect inferences. In many work environments, where there are real or perceived dangers to expressing a negative opinion about the boss' previous decisions, the kind of person who is most likely to volunteer her opinion is someone who feels positively about the issue under discussion. Many bosses are aware of the issue in theory, but it is surprisingly rare to find one who has looked at the way she herself receives feedback on a specific issue and thought about selection effects biasing which people choose to respond. In some ways, this explanation of why superiors can be so delusional is rather comforting. It posits that many instances of supervisory madness are not the result of malice or idiocy, but rather genuine unawareness due to impeded data-flows (and resultant sample selection bias).

If you find yourself in a supervisory position, you can outsmart and outperform your rivals by putting in place systems that genuinely ensure that the probability of feedback reaching you is not dependent on the values that feedback takes. There are many possible systems that could work. Anonymous comment-boxes are the right kind of idea: by disconnecting ideas from names, they stop subordinates from expecting reward or punishment depending on the value their feedback took.

However, there are often doubts about quite how anonymous an anonymous system is, and it's difficult as a supervisor to weigh the negative view on a piece of paper as strongly as the positive views you keep hearing in person. As a result, the best system is probably one that involves encouraging negative feedback in person: finding subordinates you trust and asking them what other people complain about most; encouraging a "Devil's Advocate" mentality during projects and meetings; or asking subordinates what the least-best thing about a particular project is ("yes I know you think this project is wonderful. But if you were to think it wasn't wonderful, what would you think wasn't wonderful about it?") Ultimately, your biggest strengths will be the simple awareness that negative feedback must be out there in your organisation, and the vigilance to keep looking for it despite the psychological temptation to have the positives reinforced.

When you're in the position of the supervised, rather than the supervisor, you can remind yourself of the importance of raising relevant issues with supervisors even when the issue seems obvious, when you'd previously assumed that if nothing was being done it was because the higher-ups didn't care. In the best case they may be willing to re-examine the issue once made aware of the rest of the evidence, but at the very least you can have the comfort of realising that you're not being treated with purposeful malice. Understanding statistics can be an unexpected source of inner peace.

FORGETTING FRIENDS

By contrast, the following advice may have a negative effect on your self esteem— sometimes, noticing sample selection bias can knock your sense of self importance. Just don't say I didn't warn you.

When I first got to America I noticed that a lot of people seemed to remember me long after I'd forgotten them. This led to all kinds of awkwardness, since they knew my name and where we'd met while I had no idea who they were. But it wasn't fair, I thought: of course they remembered me—I was the guy with the curious accent, and they were just one of the hundred identical Americans (sorry Americans) that I'd met that month.

I mentioned this odd phenomenon to a religious Jewish friend. "I have the same thing!," he said— "everyone remembers the kid with the Jewish head-covering, but how am I meant to distinguish all these identically-dressed hipster girls?" A short-haired female friend had a similar response: "I totally get you," she answered, "everyone remembers the short-haired girl (there's, like, five of us on campus?) but there's no way I'm going to remember them. It's not fair, it's just not fair."

By this point I was hugely suspicious that, in fact, all three of us had over-estimated how memorable we were relative to other people. On reflection, all three of us had fallen victim to sample selection bias. The problem was two different kinds of missing data. First, in our own interactions, we lack a lot of data about the times when other people forgot us. We've all had moments where we couldn't remember someone's name for the life of us, but managed to fake through a short conversation by calling them "you" or "buddy" or "heyyy!" Note that all the data with the value "I forgot your name, you remembered mine" gets back to me; I'm always awkwardly aware of it. But there are probably lots of instances when someone else forgot my name completely, spent a five-minute conversation calling me "buddy," and I just didn't notice. Strike one for sample selection bias.

The second kind of missing data is that there are endless interactions that don't involve me at all in which one party forgets the other party's name: where my religious Jewish friend, or my short-haired female friend, forgets the name of someone who remembers them. Out of the total population of forgotten-name incidents (the ones where I forget someone's name; the ones where someone forgets mine; and the ones where someone else forgets another someone-else's), the data that reaches me is overwhelmingly skewed towards the instances where someone remembers me and I don't remember them. Due to my biased sample, I wrongfully draw the inference that I'm unusually memorable (yes, yes, it's hard being a celebrity). It turns out that I'm not; everyone forgets some names and remembers others.

CONGRATULATIONS

There are many similar areas of personal life where selection bias occurs because we only experience "first person" the things that happen to us, and don't always notice that we don't receive the same stream of data for other people's first-person experiences.

When I was younger I learnt (very basic) guitar. I played mainly in my room, in the classic "awkward teenager croons melancholy love-songs" mold. Sometimes, feeling plucky, I even did Open Mic Nights. And invariably, after the show, people would come up to congratulate me and say how much they enjoyed my performance— I hate to brag but some people even said I was the best in the whole show. The first kind of selection bias here is obvious: if someone thinks you played badly, they're not too likely to tell you to your face. Almost-nobody comes up to a performer at a friendly open mic and says "hey!, I saw your performance and I just wanted to say that you're a mediocre singer and a barely-competent guitar-player," despite the fact that many open-mic guitarists are indeed mediocre and barely competent. Out of the entire population of opinions about my playing (positive opinions and negative opinions), the sample that reaches me is strongly biased towards the positive ones.

The second kind of selection bias is a little more subtle: immediately after a performance, you tend to drift away from everyone else, and don't get to count how many times each of the other performers gets told how wonderful they were. Intellectually you know this is happening, but pragmatically you forget about it. So out of the entire population of opinions about open-mic participants (the opinion that you were good; the opinion that you were bad; the opinion that someone else was good; the opinion that someone else was bad) you'll hear a lot about how good you were, almost-nothing about how bad you were, and perhaps a little of each about how good or bad other people in the show were ("that girl just before you was amazing! I mean, not as good as you, obviously. But pretty good, y'know...") The sample of opinions that reaches you is massively biased, and so you will greatly over-estimate how much other people liked your music and under-estimates how much they liked other performers'. Of course the other performers' biggest fans aren't talking to you right after the show - they've gone to talk to their own favourite musician. As a consequence, you over-estimate how good you were compared to other performers.

Constantly being aware of the extent that selection bias affects our self-perception would be disastrously depressive (I did warn about that earlier, right?) Often it's probably better for us to ignore the sample selection bias, enjoy strumming on the big stage, and gracefully accept the compliments afterwards. But if you get to the point where it feels like everyone's telling you you're an amazing musician and you could definitely make it if you went professional, it's probably good to stop and think about the selection bias in your feedback channels. Before you quit your day-job.

CHAPTER TWO:
ENDOGENEITY

THINGS CAUSE OTHER THINGS

"Endogeneity" is one of those words so thoroughly ignored that it doesn't even make it into most normal spellcheckers. This is a minor outrage, because endogeneity is one of the most useful concepts in all of statistics. It is also impossible to describe succinctly. The simple (and not necessarily helpful) definition is that something is endogenous if it is determined within the system of interest. By contrast, something is "exogenous" if it is determined by factors outside that system.

In biology, something endogenous originates within the organism, tissue or cell you're looking at; something exogenous originates outside it. The same idea applies in social science (and in everyday life), except there is no perfect equivalent to cells and tissues and organisms. But social scientific arguments are composed of models, and real life is composed of informal, implicit models: when we think about whether one thing does or doesn't cause another, we are creating an implicit mental equation with "the things doing the causing" on the left-hand side and "the things that are caused" on the right. These models are, in fact, the relevant analogues for cells or organisms in biology, and if we construct the models poorly then we run into all kinds of problems. For example, perhaps our model says that X causes Y when in fact Y causes X, or perhaps it claims that A causes B when in fact C causes both of them. Both of these are forms of endogeneity problem, for a precise reason that will be discussed later. For now, we can think of it like this: if our model claims that X causes Y, when in fact Y can cause X, then "the fact of Y causing X" is an important phenomenon that is occurring outside the logic of our model (this one is a little complicated); if our model claims that A causes B when in fact C causes both of them then C is an important phenomenon from outside our model that is influencing the outcome (this one is much simpler).

If these ideas sound familiar, perhaps that's because of the famous maxim "correlation does not imply causation." Well spotted, cunning reader: correlations masquerading as causations are indeed one type of endogeneity problem, and we'll discuss those later in the chapter.

To understand endogeneity, though, we must first understand those informal, implicit mental models. So here we go. In real life, when we see an output of interest, we in fact build a kind of model in our heads to explain how it occurred. The questions that we need to answer are basically "which inputs went in to cause this output?," and "how much influence did each of those inputs have?" The problem could be something like "why doesn't Little Mikey have any friends?;" the output of interest is "number of friends that Mikey has," which in this case is zero, and the inputs could be things like "Little Mikey keeps punching other children in the face," which has a very strong effect on the output, and "Little Mikey has this really annoying way of sneezing," which does have some impact but not quite as much. The fact that Input A has a large negative effect on the output implies that if we could reduce Input A that would increase the output accordingly; if we reduced input B, which has a smaller negative effect on the output, then the output would increase but not by as much.

As will be clear from the above paragraph, an implicit model can be written out in long-form, but it'll quickly get lost in the details and it's hard to convey the model with precision. There is a solution, but it's often less popular than Little Mikey: equations. When Stephen Hawking was writing A Brief History of Time (a life-changing read, by the way), he was told that every equation he put in it would cost him half his readership. He limited himself to one and the book sold 10 million copies, so if the warning was correct then that was a pretty expensive equation. Unfortunately there's no way I can write the next section without using equations, and lots of them. They'll be nice ones, I promise; when it comes to equations I'm as bad as anyone, and when I see them in a paper I tend to skip over as fast as my eyes will carry me. But since we all do use them (implicitly) in our everyday lives, and since they never seem to bother us there, they can't possibly be as scary as they look.

A SIMPLE IMPLICIT EQUATION

Suppose you're standing in the supermarket and trying to decide which line to join. You see a couple of families with trolleys full of food, and a couple of lonely singles with a small basket each. You make a quick mental calculation: each of the families will probably take 10 minutes to clear the line, each of the singles will probably take 5. Congratulations!, you've just created an implicit mental equation. It looks a little something like this:

$$10f + 5s = t$$

f = *no. of families in line in front of you,*
s = *no. of singles in line in front of you,*
t = *time you'll have to wait to reach the front of the line.*

That's not so bad, right? On the left we have some inputs, and on the right we have an output, and we can predict the output using some function of the inputs. We call the output the "dependent variable" because it can't vary freely within our model: its value is dependent on the values taken by the inputs. Which makes sense, because the whole point of our model was to predict the value of the output based on the values of the inputs. Similarly, we call the inputs "independent" because their variation should not be determined by any of the variables in the model. Like teenagers, independent variables won't let anyone tell them what to do or what to be.

Now, obviously there's something missing here: those "10 minutes" and "5 minutes" figures were only guesses, they weren't some kind of (impossibly precise) measure of exactly how long each person will take. We need to add something called an error term. The error term sweeps up all the random variation and represents it as a single letter. We can now write the proper implicit equation — again, you're doing something like this in your head every time you see a shopping line, whether you realise or not.

$$10f + 5s = t + e$$

f = *no. of families,*
s = *no. of singles,*
t = *time you'll have to wait,*
e = *the error term.*

This equation tells us that if there's 2 families and 3 singles in line in front of you, you can expect to wait (10 x 2) + (5 x 3) = 35 minutes, plus-or-minus the random error term. Few things in this world can be predicted with absolute certainty, and we know that some of the families will only take 7 minutes while others will take 12; some of the singles will only take 4 minutes and others 6. Often those random errors will cancel out—if someone takes a minute more than expected, and someone else takes a minute less, then you're back on track overall—but if you're unlucky you'll get stuck in a line where everyone is slower than expected. However, you know that the average total wait time will be 35 minutes, and that any variation around that will be random: while there is some probability that the wait will be longer, there is exactly the same probability that the wait will be shorter, and small differences from 35 minutes are much more probable than large ones. Now we have a proper estimate of the time we'll wait in line: 35 minutes, give or take something, but probably not much.

BEWARE THE ERROR TERM, MY CHILD!

At this point you may be sitting back smugly, wondering what all this error-related fuss is about. That was easy! But that's error terms for you, the sneaky monkeys, they start making problems when you least expect it.

In the shopping-line example, the error term was uncorrelated with the independent variables. This was why we could use the formula to predict how long we would have to wait in line—we knew that, while there would be some variation from the expected time, it would be random variation and there would be no way to predict it from what we knew previously.

We assume, by definition, that the error term is random variation — that errors are clustered around zero, that under-estimates are as probable as over-estimates, and that small errors are more probable than large ones. A model with random error in it is still a useful model — not quite as good as a perfect one, sure, but still worth a lot. Imagine if you had a model that could predict next year's prices in the stock market, plus or minus 10%. If you bought a hundred stocks that your model predicted would go up next year, you would end up making a lot of money. Some of your predictions would be over-estimates, and on those stocks you might even lose some money, but also some of your predictions would be under-estimates, and on those stocks you'd make even more than expected. As long as you bought a lot of different stocks, the random errors would cancel out and you'd end the year much richer than you started.

But what happens if the error term secretly includes factors that are not, in fact, random? If there exists any variable that is correlated with the error term then the error term is non-random — this is necessarily true, basically because of what it means to be truly random. This means that the differences between our predicted outcome and the true outcome will be systematic, not random: if you had some data about the variable that was secretly correlated with the error term, you would then be able to predict in different situations whether the model would overestimate or underestimate the output. But if our model is wrong systematically, not randomly, it is not very useful for making predictions. Imagine, for example, that your previously-discussed stock-picking algorithm systematically overestimated prices by 10% — you would stand to lose a lot of money when the prices of many of the stocks you bought go down instead of up.

As a rigorous definition, a variable is endogenous within a given system if it is correlated with the error term in the equation.

OMITTED VARIABLE BIAS

One way to destroy a model through endogeneity is to leave out an important variable that is needed to explain the outcome in question. Any part of your outcome that would have been explained by this missing variable will have to be swept into the error term, which will now be completely non-random; it will contain the entirety of the omitted variable. For example, the formula for the area of a square is (of course):

$$height \times width = area$$

where height = width. But imagine that your model of a square was simply:

$$height = area + error$$

This is a monumentally stupid formula for the area of a square, but let's run with it for now. Suppose you believed in it: you would measure a bunch of squares and notice that your formula did have some kind of truth. You'd see a strong correlation between height and area, and that the higher a square was the bigger its area tended to be. You'd predict that a square of height one should have area = 1, which is correct; that a square of height two should have area = 2, when in fact it has area = 4; and that a square of height three should have area = 3, when in fact it has area = 9. The error in your predictions is completely non-random: the error gets greater as the height gets greater, for a start, because the error "contains" the influence of the omitted variable "width." Furthermore, for any square with area greater than one, your prediction is always an under-estimate. If you gather a large set of squares then your error terms will not average out; your formula will systematically under-estimate areas.

WHY G.P.A. IS STUPID

A very important example of a model whose stated purpose is destroyed by omitted variable bias is college G.P.A. In the U.S., grades tend to be calculated on a 0-to-4 scale where an A-grade is worth 4.0, an A- is worth 3.7, a B+ is worth 3.3, and so forth. A student's overall G.P.A. is calculated as the average of her scores in all the courses she took during her degree. The reasons that G.P.A. is stupid, rigorously, are the exact same reasons that G.P.A. seems stupid intuitively: college students get to choose their own courses, and the difficulty of getting an A relates to the difficulty of the course you're in, so people who choose easier courses will get better grades. As a freshman and sophomore I didn't worry too much about G.P.A. because I assumed no-one (not employers, surely not grad schools) would be stupid enough to assign any meaning to a metric which so blatantly failed to capture what it claimed to. But hey, apparently nobody is immune from getting tricked by endogeneity.

When people treat G.P.A. as if it actually captures something meaningful — for example, when they create a G.P.A. cutoff for a job posting or a grad school application — they are implicitly assuming something like this:

$$X(f) + Y(b) = G.P.A. + error$$

$f = effort,$
$b = ability,$
X & Y are functions.

The idea is that G.P.A. is largely determined by effort and ability, plus or minus some random variation. The error term here would sweep up such factors as whether the student got woken up by a parrot at 4 a.m. the night before an exam, or whether her laptop died in the middle of writing her term paper. Those causes of variation have a very important feature: they are not correlated with a student's effort, her motivation, her deviousness, or anything else. If this model were correct then college G.P.A. would still not be a perfectly 'fair' measure, on an individual level, since some students would just be unlucky and get lower scores than their effort and ability could have achieved. On a cumulative level, however, it would be true that a student with high G.P.A. would, with high probability, possess better ability and effort than a low G.P.A. student.

Once students are allowed to pick their own courses, however, G.P.A. becomes an implausible measure of effort and ability. While it may remain true that, for any given course you take, your grades will correlate fairly well with the effort you put in and your ability at that subject, the fact that you can choose your own courses introduces an opposing force: if you choose easier courses you can exert less effort and still attain better grades. As such, G.P.A. could correlate inversely with effort.

This, then, is the root of our endogeneity problem. Our error term (the difference between the G.P.A. values 'predicted' by our first model and the actual G.P.A. outcomes) is not at all random. In fact, it is highly correlated with an omitted variable — difficulty of courses chosen. For any given level of effort and ability, taking easier courses will result in a better G.P.A. But since choosing easy courses for yourself is (probably) a sign of academic laziness and disinterest, high G.P.A. could start to correlate inversely with academic ambition and G.P.A. will not be a good predictor of ability and effort — academic laziness is itself a form of "low effort." Note that even if there are brilliant, hard-working students who get 3.8s despite taking difficult courses, they would've done even better if they had taken easier courses.

Taking into account course selection, we can see that the correct equation for G.P.A. would be more like this:

$$X(f) + Y(b) + Z(c) = G.P.A. + error$$

$f = effort,$
$b = ability,$
$c = easiness\ of\ courses\ selected,$
$X,\ Y\ \&\ Z\ are\ functions.$

This is still an over-simplification: there are a million other factors that determine G.P.A., from the all-important skill called "knowing-the-system" to the undoubtedly-influential "whether or not student already has a job-offer by senior year." But our improved, three-input equation at least shows that a high G.P.A. can be caused not only by high ability and effort, which are admirable, but also by purposefully taking easy courses, which is the-opposite-of-admirable. Someone who understands this would be reticent to draw any kind of inference from a student's G.P.A. alone; she'd see that the signal given by G.P.A. is worse than useless.

Causality Loops

A second kind of endogeneity problem occurs when cause and effect are connected by a kind of "causality loop." Endogeneity will be a problem whenever the output that you're trying to explain might also be the cause, rather than the effect, of the input that you use to explain it. When your mother tells you she shouts at you because you never come to visit her, you might retort that you don't like to visit because she's always shouting at you. "Mother," you tell her, "my visits are endogenous to how much you shout at me." Her implicit equation is:

$$A\left(\frac{1}{v}\right) = s + error$$

v = *number of times you visit,*
s = *number of times she shouts at you,*
A = *some function of* $1/v$.

In her model, the number of times she shouts at you is inversely related to the number of times you visit: the more you visit, the less she shouts. But you point out that all her shouting causes you not to visit:

$$X\left(\frac{1}{s}\right) = v + error$$

In your model, the number of times you visit is inversely related to the number of times she shouts at you. So the amount you get shouted at is endogenous to how much you visit, and the amount you visit is endogenous to how much you get shouted at. The upshot is that we can't draw any reliable inferences about how much you will visit (or be shouted at) from the models written above; we'd need to create a better model that could handle the endogeneity problem properly.

PEOPLE WHO SWITCHED

A similar problem plagues insurance advertising. Insurance firms regularly boast that "people who switched their insurance to us saved an average of $102!" This tidbit tells us exactly nothing about the probability that we would save money by switching to their insurance. The sample of people who switched insurance is massively endogenous; people who discover that they'd save a lot might switch providers, but people who discover that the new company would be more expensive for them are probably going to stay put. In a world where two insurance companies offered exactly the same average prices, with a random assortment of people finding that they could save money by switching from A to B but the same number able to save just as much by switching from B to A, both companies could honestly advertise that "people who switched their insurance to us saved an average of $X!" In terms of endogeneity, the outcome to be explained (saving money) is actually a cause of the insurance firms' explanation of that outcome (switching insurance providers), so the inference they unsubtly imply (that you, or any other random person, will probably save money by switching to their insurance) is completely false.

In some ways we should be more impressed by a company that advertised that "people who switched their insurance to us paid an average of $40 MORE." This implies that people found the product so excellent that they were willing to pay more to get it, which at least makes it worth spending some time to find out more about it.

BILL AND MARK ARE ENDOGENOUS

Endogeneity is also the reason that you should never trust anyone who tells you something like "Bill Gates and Mark Zuckerberg both dropped out of college and did very well for themselves; therefore, we need to encourage our young-folks to be more adventurous, risk-taking, entrepreneurial." Bill and Mark were not just two randomly-selected Harvard undergrads — first, the fact that they dropped out of college was endogenously determined by their personalities, which also affected their probability of success; second, the fact that they are known about by the person giving the example is itself endogenous to their later successes.

For Bill and Mark, part of the endogeneity was from personality. What kind of person drops out of Harvard aged 20? Well, suffice to say that it's not an ordinary Harvard undergrad, given the graduation rate. In a world where dropping out of college is a big taboo, and where going to Harvard is kind-of-a-big-deal, the sort of person who drops out of Harvard is not an ordinary sort of person at all (or an ordinary sort of Harvard undergrad, which is far from the same thing). Bill and Mark probably both had some extraordinary personality traits — boldness, courage, hacking ability, self-belief — which helped them greatly in their business careers, and which made them willing to drop out of Harvard.

In Mark's case there was an additional source of drop-out-decision endogeneity: he already had a pretty successful company, with Silicon Valley offices and Peter Thiel's investment, before he officially dropped out of school. The omitted variable — whether or not your company is already mind-blowingly successful — is surely correlated to the probability that you'll decide to drop out of college, and your decision to drop out of college will then seem to have more of a positive influence on your successes than it really should. People who just note that Mark was a risk-taking college dropout, but fail to note that he was already massively successful before he dropped out, will over-estimate the benefit of dropping out for those without an already-successful company.[iv]

The first type of endogeneity problem, discussed above, occurs at the level of deciding to drop out. But there is a second endogeneity problem that occurs at the level of people-discussing-college-dropouts. Most college dropouts are not well-known enough that strangers would discuss them when talking about college dropouts. Imagine if your Cousin Frank abandoned Harvard and went on to live in his girlfriend's garage for the rest of his life, running a failed internet startup. You would know about Cousin Frank's misadventures, and the rest of Frank's family would, and some of his high-school friends. Let's say, generously, that 1,000 people would be aware of Frank's dropout status and his unsuccessful existence (maybe through reading his facebook updates). By contrast, millions and millions of people know about Mark Zuckerberg's story, how he dropped out of Harvard and became a billionaire: 20 million officially saw the Zuckerberg biopic The Social Network, and 500 million have accounts with his website. Taking the low-ball 20 million figure, for every one Mark Zuckerberg there could be 20,000 Cousin Franks, and (if none of the Cousin Franks had any mutual friends, which is a stupid assumption but let it slide for now) then the 20 million people who knew of one Mark Zuckerberg and one Cousin Frank might assume that college dropouts had a 50/50 chance of becoming billionaires. Not bad odds, I'd say. But of course this calculation is junk: the 'actual' odds (in our artificial example) would be 1 / 20,001. Not so hot.

CONSULTANTS

If endogeneity can fool ordinary people, it can also apparently fool huge multinational companies. A leading American management-consulting firm has a prominent graph on its website showing how their clients' share-price gains since 1980 have outperformed a stock-market index by a factor of four. This looks pretty impressive, unless you think about it. There's two endogeneity effects here. First, the kind of client who tries to hire a consultant is not representative of companies as a whole — perhaps the companies who hire consultants have more dynamic leadership to begin with; perhaps the future's looking bright for them, and they feel that they have cash to spare; or perhaps they were doing unusually poorly, needed restructuring, but were about to bottom-out anyway. Second, the clients that a consulting firm accepts are not a random sample either: a consulting firm may only take on clients that it thinks it can help, or perhaps even that it thinks will have share-price gains in future years (as opposed to one that will still do badly, but perhaps less-badly, with the consultants' help). If the consulting firm had randomised which clients it accepted and which it didn't, the difference in share price gains between the accepted and rejected firms would provide a meaningful gauge of the consultants' contribution. The statistics presented on the website, however, tells us more about who hires consultants than about how much consultants help companies.

SOCIAL SCIENCE AND NATURAL SCIENCE

One of the great problems of social science is that nothing ever sits still. Modern statistics got its big break with 1920s agricultural experiments: you take two nearby rows of corn and treat them with two different fertilizers, and at the end of the season you see which field grew better. The early years in the development of statistics were largely about figuring out the quality of inferences you can make from data: how do you tell if the different yields were caused by a better fertiliser or by a fluke? How many ears of corn do you need to check before you can confidently declare the characteristics of the entire field? These are difficult questions, and it took some obscenely smart people to provide rigorous answers. But one comfort we had was that the direction of causality was completely clear. The independent variable (which fertiliser you used) would affect the dependent variable (how much corn grew), but there was absolutely no way that the dependent variable (corn growth) could influence the independent variable (which of the fertilisers you had already used on it).

With humans involved, nothing is ever so simple. Suppose you're interested in primary schooling in developing countries, and want to see the effects that donating textbooks has on the students' educational outcomes. You find a village with two identical schools in it and give textbooks only to the students in School A. So far, so good: you have an independent variable (whether a student got a textbook) and a dependent variable (the students' educational outcomes at the end of the study). But unlike corn-stalks, children can move. If they (or their parents) start to realise that one school is getting better resources than the other, some of the more ambitious students might try to move across. The end of the study arrives and the students in School A achieved better academic outcomes. But did the textbooks cause the better outcomes, or did the more ambitious students cause themselves to get given textbooks? How much of the gains are due to each cause? It's hard to tell. The supposedly-dependent variable has started influencing the supposedly-independent ones. Cause and effect have become difficult to disentangle.

In fact, endogeneity plagues all kinds of social science research, and many of the social science questions that make it into the news. If you see a piece of social science reported in the media, one of your first questions should probably be "is there an endogeneity problem here?" This is not necessarily the first question you should ask about social science research in general, but there seems to be a kind of endogeneity problem with the kind of social science that gets reported in the media, namely that the kind of papers that make it into the news are unusually likely to suffer from endogeneity problems. To a stats nerd, this passes as pretty funny.

NOT ALL THAT CORRELATES IS CAUSED

If there's one statistical maxim which is widely known among non stats-nerds it's "correlation does not imply causation." Correlation means, roughly, that two variables are inter-dependent: if one goes up, the other goes up with it. (If two variables are inversely correlated then as one goes up, the other goes down). Causation means, well, that one caused the other to happen. But two variables can be correlated without any causal relationship between them: it could just be coincidence, or it could be that they are both caused by an invisible third factor. Just because two things vary together does not mean one caused the other.

A classic example of "correlation does not imply causation" is the famous story that ice-cream sales over the course of a year tend to correlate with the number of drownings. Does this mean that, say, eating ice-cream causes significant groups of children to go sugar-crazy and fall in a lake? Or, even more bizarrely, that while people are drowning they suddenly consume a lot of ice-cream? Well, unsurprisingly, no. Ice-cream sales tend to go up in summer, a time when people also spend more time swimming outdoors, so rising ice-cream sales and increased drownings are both caused by warmer weather but aren't actually related directly.

If you think this is silly and that no-one would make such a basic causation-and-correlation mistake: needless to say, think again. Public Health experts in the 1940s noticed a correlation between polio cases and ice-cream consumption, and recommended renouncing ice-cream to avoid polio. It later emerged that —you guessed it— polio outbreaks were more common in summer, and ice-cream eating was more common in summer, and polio and ice-cream had nothing to do with each other.[v]

Another great example is that the average price of rum is strongly correlated with the average wages of kindergarten-teachers. Do rising childcare wages give more spare cash to exasperated teachers, bidding up rum prices? Or do higher rum prices cause people to drink less, therefore work harder, therefore spend more money on their children's kindergartens? Neither, obviously: the price of basically-everything rises over time due to inflation, and this extraneous factor affects kindergarten-teachers' wages and rum prices and the cost of houses and MPs' salaries and almost-everything else. You can show correlation between any two price-rises and, if you're a devious sort of person, ignore the fact that both increases are caused by an invisible third factor, the general fact that prices tend to rise over time. In fact, lots of trends tend to increase over time, and if you want to get really silly you can start to point out correlations between any two such variables, ignoring the invisible third factor (that many things increase over time, in general).

A well-known newspaper once wrote about a "striking correlation" between the number of miles driven per licensed American driver and U.S. obesity rates six years later— the hypothesis was that when Americans drove more they exercised less, and (following a time-lag to allow for the change to affect physiques) they got fat. The newspaper, although straining to note that "these predictions come with a strong caveat: correlation does not equal causation," nonetheless seemed very impressed at the "near-perfect correlation." A famous economist, Justin Wolfers, went one better and showed an even-better correlation between American obesity rates and his age. As Wolfers writes: "I'm not arguing that my aging is causing higher obesity. Rather, when you see a variable that follows a simple trend, almost any other trending variable will fit it: miles driven, my age, the Canadian population, total deaths, food prices, cumulative rainfall, whatever."[vi]

CORRELATION, CAUSATION AND ENDOGENEITY

At this point, the astute reader might be wondering to herself: "couldn't all the above examples be expressed as endogeneity problems?" At which the proud author would sob loudly into his laptop, and tell everyone who would listen about how quickly Astute Reader had grown up, and wasn't it only yesterday she was browsing the introduction? Yes, correlation-is-not-causation is a specific example of an endogeneity problem. Take ice-cream and drownings. Our original (incorrect) formula was:

$$A(ice\ cream\ sales) = drownings + error$$

Our omitted variable was "outdoor temperature," which we've lumped into our error term but which is in fact correlated with both ice-cream sales and drownings. The correct formulas would be (something like):

$$Y(temperature) = ice\ cream\ sales + error$$
and
$$Z(temperature) = drownings + error$$

with any apparent connection between ice-cream sales and drownings actually driven by the common independent variable "outdoor temperature." Correlation is not causation: both outcomes are endogenous to an omitted variable that has been wrongly lumped into the error term.

CHAPTER THREE:
BAYES

You come home early one day to find that your girlfriend, who told you she was going home because she wasn't feeling well, actually snuck out to have dinner with her ex. (I hate to be the one to tell you this, but really, you had to know). What is the probability that she's cheating on you? More importantly: how should you calculate the probability that she's cheating on you? What factors do you need to take into account? You won't, and shouldn't, assign numbers here; they'd be thoroughly arbitrary ("Honey, there seems to be a 23.97% probability that you're cheating on me. Plus or minus 0.01%"). But since you're going to make an implicit probabilistic assessment anyway ("She's definitely cheating on me;" "I think she might be cheating on me;" "I'm only slightly worried that she's cheating on me;" etc. etc.), you might as well make the assessment well.

The question here is something called a conditional probability, that is, the probability of X given Y — here, the probability that she's cheating given that she snuck off to dine with her ex. So long as two things are in some way related, the conditional probability for X given Y will not be the same as the simple probability of X all on its own. For instance, the simple probability that a randomly-chosen burrito is going to be tasty might be 0.4. The conditional probability that it's going to be tasty given that your friend recommended this particular restaurant might be 0.8 — her recommendation is a non-random indicator of burrito quality. And the conditional probability that the burrito will be tasty given that your friend recommended the place, and that you've previously eaten quesadillas here and they were excellent, and that it won some prestigious burrito-making award, might be 0.99. Statisticians use the symbol $P(X|Y)$ to represent the probability of X happening given that Y did; the vertical bar represents the phrase "given that."

Now to return to our girlfriend-problem. We have a hypothesis about the world (the hypothesis that she might be cheating on us) and a new piece of evidence (she snuck off to dinner without telling us). The Reverend

Thomas Bayes was an 18th Century British clergyman who figured out exactly how to deal with these kinds of problems, where we want to know the probability that our hypothesis (that is, our causal explanation for why something happened) is correct given a new piece of evidence (that is, something that has happened). Bayes' insight was that the conditional probability P(Hypothesis|Evidence) depends on four different things—well, they're kind of connected so there's not technically four of them, but let's call it four different things for now.

First, P(Hypothesis|Evidence) depends on the probability P(Evidence|Hypothesis): if a piece of evidence was extremely probable under a given hypothesis, the existence of the evidence makes it more probable that the hypothesis was correct. This makes sense: if our hypothesis strongly predicted that a particular piece of evidence would show up, and that piece of evidence does indeed show up, then it is a little more probable that our hypothesis was correct (because if our hypothesis had predicted a particular piece of evidence, and that evidence had not shown up, then we'd be forced to conclude that our hypothesis was probably wrong).

Second, it depends on the probability that the hypothesis was correct before we saw the new evidence; statisticians call this the "prior probability." New evidence can be used to help "update" our beliefs — that is, after seeing a new piece of evidence, our previous hypothesis can become more or less probable. But we must never forget the prior probability that we started with. If the star striker on your favourite soccer team gets injured—new evidence—then it becomes less probable than it had been that your team will win the next match. However, the absolute probability that they will win the next match is still very dependent on how good they are, and how good the other team is, and how probable their win was before the injury came along. The new evidence (the striker's injury) can only cause to update our prior beliefs; it doesn't act in a vacuum, and couldn't possibly tell us how probable a win is in the absence of prior beliefs.

The third and fourth factors for the Bayesian analysis are mirrors of the first two, but with regards to the alternative hypotheses that compete with our own one to explain the world around us. The alternative hypotheses are all the other possible ways to explain what happened; all the things apart from our hypothesis that could have caused the evidence to arise. For example, perhaps you go to a neighbours house and the family dog jumps up and licks you. "The dog is licking me!," you exclaim; "this new evidence supports my hypothesis that the dog really likes me." But as a good statistician you must also consider alternative hypotheses: for example, that the dog licks everyone, or that your aftershave smells like meat. These alternatives, and many others, could also explain the evidence you're seeing.

The third factor, then, is the probability of the new evidence given the alternative hypotheses, and the fourth factor is the prior probabilities of each of the alternative hypotheses. Essentially, the same arguments as above apply in reverse: the more probable the evidence under alternative hypotheses, and the more probable those hypotheses were to begin with, the more probable it is that the new evidence has appeared due to these alternative causes, and so the less probable it is that our original hypothesis is correct. Conversely, the new evidence argues much more strongly for our initial hypothesis if the piece of evidence is highly improbable under the reasonable alternative hypotheses, or if those alternative hypotheses were initially very improbable.

Don't worry if that all seemed confusing, or if you're not sure you absorbed what you just read; unfortunately Bayes Theorem' is just one of those things you have to chew on for a while before it makes sense. Let's look at a more concrete example. Suppose that a note shows up on my desk purporting to reveal a secret crush from the most beautiful girl in the class. It is indeed somewhat-probable that the girl would send such a message if she had a crush on me: P(message | crush) is moderately-high. Depending on how attractive I am, perhaps P(crush) — the probability that she really does have a crush on me — is also non-negligible. Unfortunately, there are still the alternative hypotheses to consider: for example, that my friends are playing a prank. The probability that I would receive such a message if my friends were playing a prank — P(message | prank) — is fairly high, and the probability that my friends would play a prank on me, P(prank), is extremely high. This means that, overall, the existence of the message becomes weak evidence for the hypothesis that the girl has a crush on me; the alternative hypotheses explain the evidence just as well, and were more probable before the evidence showed up.

FORMULA FOR BAYES

Reverend Bayes was in fact the source for more than this little theorem: his work was the cornerstone for an entire statistical philosophy commonly known as (this is going to shock you) Bayesian Statistics. There is an enormous amount of controversy in the statistics world about whether Bayesianism is really the correct way to think about probabilities, as opposed to another school of thought called Frequentism, and if you ever find yourself at a statistics conference you must promise (promise!) not to mention that this book flagrantly side-stepped the Bayesian-Frequentist debate — this is one of those questions that inspires an enormous amount of passion and argument from the people who really care about it. For our purposes, though, the philosophical debate is not critical: Bayes' Theorem is a great tool for thinking about probabilities, regardless of deeper questions about the true nature of probabilities in our universe. Bayes' Theorem can be expressed as a simple formula; take a deep breath, it's honestly (honestly!) not as bad as it looks:

$$P(Hypothesis_1 \mid Evidence) =$$

$$\frac{P(Evidence \mid Hypothesis_1)P(Hypothesis_1)}{P(Evidence)}$$

$P(X)$ = the probability of X occurring,
$P(X \mid Y)$ = the probability of X occurring given that Y occurred.

What does that mean? Well, let's return to our example with the note from the beautiful girl (I liked that example). Our Hypothesis₁ was that I received the note because the girl had a crush on me, and the probability we're trying to assess is $P(H_1 \mid E)$: the probability that she really does have a crush on me given that I received the note. $P(E \mid H_1)$ was the probability that she would send the note if she had the crush; $P(H_1)$ was the probability that she had a crush on me before we knew the note existed. $P(E)$ is the total probability of seeing the evidence under all possible hypotheses; we get it by adding together $P(E \mid H_1)P(H_1)$ and $P(E \mid H_2)P(H_2)$ and $P(E \mid H_3)P(H_3)$, etc. etc., until we have gone through all the reasonable alternative hypotheses: the total probability of seeing the evidence is a function of how probable the evidence was in each possible state of the world, weighted by how probable that state of the world was to begin with, so we arrive at $P(E)$ by summing $P(E \mid H)P(H)$ for all possible H's. It is crucial that we include our own hypothesis, H_1, in the calculation of $P(E)$ — after all, our hypothesis is one of the relevant states of the world under which the new evidence might occur.

ASSIMILATING EVIDENCE

Now that we know the formula, we can start to explore its consequences. We know that there are four elements to consider when thinking about a conditional probability: the probability of E given H_1; the prior probability for H_1; the probability of E given H_{others}; and the prior probabilities for H_{others}. As previously discussed, if $P(E \mid H_1)$ rises then $P(H_1 \mid E)$ also rises; this makes sense, because the more probable the new evidence under our hypothesis, the more that seeing the new evidence makes our hypothesis more probable itself. If the prior probability $P(H_1)$ rises then the posterior probability $P(H_1 | E)$ also rises; this makes sense, because the higher the hypothesis' probability was to begin with, the higher it will be after any given piece of new evidence is introduced. Conversely, if $P(E | H_{others})$ rises then the posterior probability $P(H_1 | E)$ falls; this makes sense, because the more probable the new evidence is under the alternative hypotheses, the less the existence of the new evidence makes us certain that our Hypothesis$_1$ was correct. Finally, if the posterior probability $P(H_{others})$ rises then the posterior probability $P(H_1 | E)$ falls; this makes sense, because the more probable the alternative hypotheses were to begin with, the more probable they will be after our new evidence arrives, and so the less support the new evidence provides for our own original hypothesis — the new evidence might be proof, instead, that one of the other hypotheses was correct.

These behaviours have a number of useful consequences. One is that, even if our hypothesis is extremely improbable under a given set of evidence, our belief in it should increase if all other hypotheses are now even more improbable. Sherlock Holmes said that "when you have eliminated the impossible, whatever remains, however improbable, must be the truth;"[vii] what he was really saying was that, "If $P(E | H_{others})=0$, H_1 is correct even if $P(E | H_1)$ is very small." (Why that phrasing didn't go in the Holmes books is a mystery only to me). One example is the way that physicists developed a new model of the atom in 1909 following the famous Geiger-Marsden experiments, where a stream of alpha particles were fired at a sheet of gold foil and some of the particles were deflected backwards. In the words of Ernest Rutherford, this result was, under the prevalent model of the atom at the time, "almost as incredible as if you fired a 15-inch shell at a piece of tissue paper and it came back and hit you"— that is to say, functionally impossible. Even if the new "Rutherford Model" of the atom seemed implausible to many at the time, it became widely accepted because the same experimental results which were impossible under alternative hypotheses were at least comprehensible under the Rutherford's. After eliminating the impossible, whatever remains, plausible or implausible, must be the truth.[viii]

A second consequence is that whenever we look at how probable a new piece of evidence is under our hypothesis, we have to look at how probable the same evidence is under plausible alternative hypotheses (and how plausible those hypotheses were in the first place). We all know people who fail terribly at this: they get a certain idea in their heads, and then whenever new evidence arrives they proclaim loudly that the evidence exactly supports their original hypothesis, ignoring the fact that the same evidence also supports alternative hypotheses. These people can be even more annoying to deal with than someone who's outright wrong — the evidence does support their hypothesis, they're just being incredibly blinkered about alternative explanations. It's very hard to think enough in the middle of a debate to explain why their assertions don't actually prove their conclusion, but Bayes' Theorem shows the proper way forward.

GRAPHICAL BAYES

As we did with selection bias at the start of this book, it's possible to represent Bayes Theorem in a graphical way that may be helpful when thinking about the issue. Once again, this is an 'unofficial' and informal way to think about a statistical topic—if the approach is helpful for you then certainly make the most of it, but don't feel worried if it doesn't make sense to you. For our example, let's look at the burrito problem we looked at earlier: how good can we expect a given burrito to be, given that we chose it at random? The prior probability of a randomly chosen burrito being good, we said, was 0.4, as we can see in the graphic below. Out of any ten randomly-chosen burrito bars, we'd expect to find four out of ten serving good burritos and six out of ten serving bad ones. If our town has 120 burrito-bars overall, we expect 48 to be good (that's four-tenths of 120) and 72 to be bad (that's six-tenths of 120).

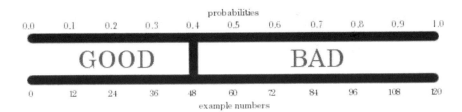

Next, we said we received new information from our friend's recommendation. Specifically, let's say that the probability that our friend recommends a place *given* that it's good is one out of two; the probability that she recommends a place *given* that it's bad is one out of twelve. (Why is our friend recommending *any* bad burrito bars? Maybe she has different taste from us, or she made a mistake, or she had a freak good burrito at generally bad burrito bar, etc). Therefore, we can colour one-half of the good burrito-bars in grey (representing that our friend recommended these burrito-bars) and colour one-twelfth of the bad burrito bars in grey (representing that our friend recommended these ones, even though they're bad). The shading makes sense when you think about it: there's a one out of two chance that our friend would recommend a place *given* that it serves good burritos, so if we separate out the good burrito bars and shade one out of two of them then we've represented that concept graphically. The same idea makes us separate out the bad burrito bars and shade one out of twelve of them.

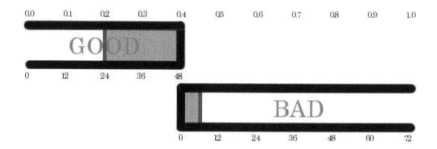

What we're really interested in now is not the probability that a randomly-chosen burrito bar is good or bad; we're interested only in the probability that a *burrito bar that our friend recommended* is good or bad. Since only the grey-highlighted burrito bars were recommended by our friend, we can simply ignore the rest of the data (the un-highlighted burrito bars, the ones that are still white). Looking only at the grey sections, we can see that their 'size' is a combination of the proportion of good (bad) burrito bars in the entire population and the proportion of good (bad) burrito bars among the ones our friend recommends for us. Since out town has 120 burrito bars and 48 are good, we expect our friend to recommend 24 of the good ones (that's one-half of 48); meanwhile, since the town has 72 bad burrito bars, we expect our friend to recommend 6 of the bad ones (that's one-twelfth of 72). So our newly relevant population would contain 30 burrito bars overall, of which 24 would be good and 6 would be bad:

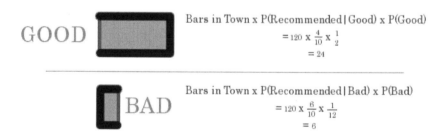

Bars in Town x P(Recommended | Good) x P(Good)
$$= 120 \times \frac{4}{10} \times \frac{1}{2}$$
$$= 24$$

Bars in Town x P(Recommended | Bad) x P(Bad)
$$= 120 \times \frac{6}{10} \times \frac{1}{12}$$
$$= 6$$

Then, if we stick these pieces together, we can consider the good/bad balance among the now-relevant universe of burritos — burritos from restaurants that our friend recommended — and get something that looks like this:

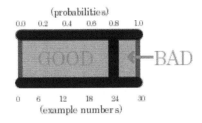

From here we can see that P(Good | Recommended) — that is, the probability a burrito is good given that our friend recommended it — will be 0.8, as we said in the text. Out of 30 burrito-bars that our friend recommends, 24 will be good and 6 will be bad; 24 out of 30 equals 4 out of 5 equals 0.8. If we compare the before-and-after graphics (see below) — before and after our friend made her recommendation — we can see what happens: we are now dealing with a smaller total population of burrito bars, and figuring out the proportion of good and bad burritos from within this smaller population instead of from within the original total. This is the essence of Bayes: figuring out the probability of seeing a particular piece of evidence *given* a particular hypothesis. We use the hypothesis to 'cut down' the original population of data to only the segment that fits the hypothesis, and then we figure out the probability of seeing the evidence within this newly narrowed-down sample.

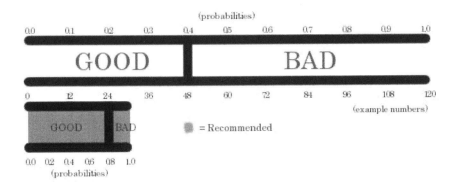

And that, visually, is Bayes Theorem in action. As with the earlier chapter on selection bias, this visualisation method is just one informal way to get your head around an abstract concept — these kinds of graphics aren't a common way to think about statistics, and if the approach doesn't make sense to you then you should feel more than free to ignore it.

BASE RATES AND VACCINATIONS

While knowing how to update beliefs based on new evidence is always important, the very concept of updating assumes that you have some "prior belief" to update from. If you incorrectly identify the prior probability, your conclusions will be incorrect even if you perform the update process correctly. Another name for a prior is a base rate, the name which is used in the psychology and behavioural-economics literatures, and so the mistake of neglecting the prior probability has come to be known as the base rate fallacy.

The famous behavioural-economics story about the base rate fallacy—it shows up in almost-every book on the topic, and I don't want other books to think this book is weird—goes as follows: a group of mysterious space-zombies have recently attacked a small village in Iowa. There is a short latency period before people outwardly manifest their zombie-ism, and we have recently developed a medical test for it that has 99% accuracy (ok, I admit it: the story isn't always told about a zombie-disease specifically. But, same idea). For these kinds of tests there are two kinds of "accurate": sensitivity, which means the probability that person who has been zombie-bitten will be correctly identified as a zombie, and specificity, which means the probability that a person who hasn't been zombie-bitten will be correctly identified as non-zombie. Let's say our test has both 99% specificity and 99% sensitivity. Sounds pretty impressive, right? But thankfully, till now, zombie-bites are very rare: only 1% of the population have been bitten. If we have successfully isolated the 1000 people in the village and tested them for zombie-ism, how many of the people who test positive for zombie-bite have actually been bitten by a zombie?

The unthinking answer is "99%" — the test is 99% accurate, after all, both 99% sensitive and 99% specific. But the truth is very different. Zombie-bites are very, very rare — of our 1000 people, only 10 have actually been bitten. They all get identified when we administer the test (probably: there's some random variation here, but we won't go into it). But among the 990 people who haven't been bitten, on average 1% (or roughly 9.9 people, so in most cases 10 people) will get a "false positive" and would be identified as zombies when they actually weren't. Our test is indeed 99% accurate, but due to the base rates (a very low base rate of zombies; a very high base rate of non-zombies) we still wind up with 10 correctly-identified zombies and 10 non-zombies wrongly identified as zombies. Only 50% of people who get a positive test are actually, genuinely undead.

The base rate fallacy occurs when you neglect to take account of the base rate, the prior probability that something was true before new evidence was introduced. In the case of the zombie-test, the fallacy is to forget that the base rate probability (i.e., the probability that a randomly-selected person has been bitten, before any tests are run) is incredibly low. The test result does give us new evidence: if it comes out positive, that gives us a clue as to whether the person is zombie-bitten or not. But that clue is only going to guide us well if we consider it in the context of the base rate. Our final question has to be "what is the probability that the person is zombifying, given that the test came out positive, and given that the test is pretty good but also that it isn't perfect, and given that non-zombies greatly outnumber zombies in our target population?" This is kind of a mouthful, but it gets the answer right..

Note that things would be very different if we looked at a population with a different base-rate of zombies. Suppose we hadn't reached the village fast enough and by the time we got there, say, 50% of the population were already zombies (and 50% weren't). You could then safely claim that if a patient's test came back positive there was a 99% probability that she was a zombie: specifically, if we tested 1,000 people, 500 zombies would take the test and 495 would correctly test positive (that's 99% of them), while 500 not-zombies would take the test and 5 would falsely test positive (that's 1%), so 495/500 positive test results would be from zombies—which, of course, is still 99%. In that case, the base rate fallacy would (accidentally) not apply because the base rate would be completely uninformative: taking a randomly-selected person who had not been given the test, we would have no reason to suspect whether she was or wasn't zombie-bitten (both would be equally probable), and therefore any information we gleaned from running the test would be the only relevant information for our later calculations.

SALLY CLARK

You might be thinking that the example above is convoluted, and unlikely, and a variety of other things (even if you imagine it had been about a real medical condition, rather than zombies). But the public ignorance of the base rate fallacy has important and tragic consequences. Many doctors have trouble with the base rate fallacy — one landmark study found that only 15% of doctors gave the correct answer when presented with a base rate question like the one above, which has scary implications for medical decision-making.[ix] Very few people in the general population have internalised the right way to think about these probabilities, and it is not intuitively an obvious way to do things. One of the most awful consequences of this unfamiliarity was the Sally Clark trial.

Sally Clark was a British mother who was put on trial after two of her children died of the same rare affliction, Sudden Infant Death Syndrome (SIDS). The prosecution's argument was that, since only 1 in 8,543 children die of SIDS, the probability that two children in the same family would succumb to it was 1 in 8,543² — that is, one in seventy-three million. This, on its own, was an absurd leap: you can only multiply probabilities together in this way if the two events are completely independent, such that whether or not one of them occurs has no influence on whether the other does. But this is a crazy assumption when you're talking about medical conditions; many such conditions run in families, and if someone else in your family suffers from one then the probability that you will suffer from it is immensely heightened.

The second mistake the prosecutors made — the base rate mistake — was to only look at one part of a conditional probability in question and completely fail to look at the others. The prosecutors argued to the jury as follows: the probability that two children in the same family would die of SIDS is extremely low. Since it is so improbable that the two Clark children died of SIDS, and the only other explanation in the circumstances was that they were murdered by their mother, they must have been murdered by their mother. But the prosecutors failed to take into account the alternative hypotheses, and their probabilities. It is also extremely improbable that a mother would murder her own children — it's just not something that mothers tend to do. The correct way to estimate whether the children had died of SIDS would be as follows:

$$P(S \mid D) =$$

$$\frac{P(D \mid S)P(S)}{P(D \mid M)P(M) + P(D \mid S)P(S) + P(D \mid O)P(O)}$$

S = *Two young siblings die of SIDS*,
D = *Two young siblings die in infancy*,
M = *Two young siblings murdered by their mother*,
O = *Two young siblings die in infancy for any other reasons*.

The prosecutors were right that the probability of two siblings dying of SIDS was very low, and that the product $P(D \mid S)P(S)$ was very low overall: $P(S)$, in the abstract, was very low, so multiplying it with $P(D \mid S)$, which is equal to 1 by definition (if the two young siblings die of SIDS then they certainly died), gives a very low number. But the prosecutors ignored the fact that the bottom half of the equation is also a very small number: $P(M)$ is incredibly low, as are the probabilities for any other possible explanations. A very small number divided by a slightly-larger-but-still-very-small number gives a relatively high probability overall. So while P(S) is very low, P(S|D) is not low at all, and certainly not low enough to conclude that the children must have been murdered. An innocent woman, who had just lost two young children, went to jail because no-one in the courtroom spotted the base rate fallacy being committed.[x]

CHOOSING JOBS

While obviously less important, there are many more examples of the base rate fallacy that are far more commonplace. A very talented friend of mine was in the envious position of choosing between job offers at the three leading companies in her field. One of the reasons she gave for her eventual choice was that the firm she selected got more analysts than any other into Harvard Business School. This was, strictly, true. But it was actually irrelevant to her purposes (which were to get into HBS) because the firm was also significantly larger than its competitors. The proportion of analysts who were accepted to HBS was in fact almost identical among the three major firms. (The cunning reader will see that there are also endogeneity problems here — did the analysts at the top companies get into HBS because they'd worked at the top companies, or because they were so marvelously talented that they could get into the top companies and HBS? Well spotted, cunning reader). Written like this, the mistake seems obvious — surely you'd notice something like that while making a big decision like choosing a job? But it's hard to be forever on-guard for the base rate fallacy; until you really build it into your way of thinking, you won't notice it when it really counts.

SEXUALITY

Another friend recently explained her theory to me about how to guess whether someone was gay or not based on their facebook profile. (I'm going to take a parenthesis here to note my general dislike of the pastime of guessing whether people are gay or not, and not just because I think it's statistically invalid). She then tried to prove her theory by showing me a series of facebook profiles belonging to gay friends and pointing out that every one of them conformed to the theory. Now, there's actually a logical fallacy here: you can never prove that, say, "all the hipsters in the world are at this party" by looking at the people at the party and showing that they're all hipsters; you'd also need to show that everybody *not* at the party was not a hipster, otherwise it may be the case that some hipsters are at the party and others are not. But there's also a statistical fallacy, namely the base rate fallacy. Suppose that 10% of the population is gay — scientific estimates range from about 3% to about 20%, but we will go with 10% for now. Even if every single gay person's profile conformed to the standard my friend described, and only one-ninth of straight people's profiles did, 50% of profiles that fit the standard would be of straight people and 50% would be of gay people. The test is not very useful if you want to know whether someone is gay.

This, of course, generalises. A lot of college students spend a lot of time guessing whether other students are gay or not — it's perhaps the second-most popular college pastime, behind trying to figure out whether someone fancies you. But again, for any trait that you think is 9x more common among the gay population, if 90% of the population is straight then 50% of your results will be "false positives." And many straight people are regularly misidentified as gay as a result. The next time somebody tells you that so-and-so is definitely gay because (s)he dresses/acts/talks a certain way, tell them about the base rate fallacy then gracefully change the topic.

GENIUS ISN'T EVERYWHERE

The base rate fallacy is also one-among-many reasons that parents misidentify their kids as possible geniuses. Frankly, in this situation, the statistical fallacy itself is probably massively secondary to wishful thinking: the parent wants to think that his child is special, and the particular fallacy used to reach that conclusion is probably unimportant. Nonetheless, the base rate fallacy is in effect. It may be true that one of Einstein's teachers told his father that the boy would never amount to anything.[xi] It is also true that lots of other students are told they aren't very bright, and that they'll never amount to anything. But the base rate of Einstein-esque geniuses is probably pretty low, whatever Einstein's genius actually consisted of. As such, even if 100% of geniuses struggled in school and only 10% of regular students did, there are so many more regular students in the world that any particular struggling student is most-probably not a genius. (If any parents are reading this: it doesn't apply to your little tyke, of course — she's definitely the next Einstein).

DATING BASE RATES

Finally, base rates also shed new light on why some people who really don't deserve it seem to get a lot of dates. The truth is, you rarely get to see someone else's "base rate" for dating — which is to say, we get to see who other people end up dating, but we don't get to see how many people they asked out before the dates who said yes said yes. The probability that someone will date you if you don't ask (or tell him you like him, or lean in for the kiss, or...) is pretty low, so the prior probability of getting a date is largely dependent on how many people you try with. Only after that does it matter how many of those people say yes. But if we neglect the base rate, we assume that anyone with lots of dates was very attractive to others (that is, getting a high proportion of "yesses," when in fact she may simply have been making a lot of attempts. The same goes for people who seem unusually successful at pulling off "pick-ups" in clubs — some of them may really be able to walk into a club and pick-up anybody they set their eye on, but many are making a whole lot of failed attempts before hitting any successes. Which puts a different gloss on things than they often like to present.

CODA

Well, here we are, it's the end of the book. Doesn't time fly? Along the way we've learnt that:

- Selection bias is everywhere, and creeps up on us whenever we take a non-random sample and act as if it were random. Some data is so sneaky that it biases itself: whether or not a particular piece of data arrives in your final sample is dependent on the value that datum would've taken. This problem caused pollsters to miss-call President Truman's re-election,and corrupts the data in the U.S. Census. On an everyday-life level, it stops bosses from getting proper feedback from their subordinates, causes us to overestimate how memorable we are to others, and makes every performer think she was the best at the open mic.

- Endogeneity problems occur whenever the supposedly-random error term turns out to be correlated with a variable in your (implicit) model, or with one that should've been in your model, but wasn't. This problem renders college G.P.A. completely useless as a measure of ability, invalidates the advertising claims of insurance companies and management consultants, and makes Gates and Zuckerberg terrible examples of the college dropout. Endogeneity lies behind some big problems in social science, and the famous dictum that correlation does not imply causation.

- Bayes' Theorem helps us update our old beliefs based on new evidence. The theorem shows why Rutherford's new model of the atom became accepted, and why it's difficult to accurately test whether someone's a zombie. Public misunderstanding of Bayes had horrifically tragic consequences in the Sally Clark trial. The theorem explains why raw business-school placement numbers are irrelevant when choosing jobs, and why you can't actually tell if someone's gay by looking at their facebook profile. Bayes explains why being bad at school doesn't imply you're the next Einstein, and why self-styled "pick up artists" might not be quite as suave as they think.

Not bad for a couple of hours' reading I'd say. "Still, can you summarise each chapter in a single sentence?," I hear you ask. Wow, you've really got a short attention span huh? Ok, here we go:

• Always check that all the information you need has reached you, and that the data that's missing isn't missing according to the value it would have taken.

• Make sure your implicit model contains all the relevant variables, and that any error left over is truly random and not secretly correlated with your inputs or with omitted variables.

• Update your probabilistic assessments based on new information, but don't forget the initial probabilities of different hypotheses.

And there it is, the essence of statistics. I lie, of course: statistics is a dense and wondrous forest, and there's very much more to learn and explore—if you'd like some Recommended Readings, just turn to the next page. But this is the end of the heart of this book; thanks for reading, it's been great seeing you. Never forget: there is nothing sexier than a stats nerd.

RECOMMENDED READING

There's a number of great "popular statistics" books out there. One group of books gives simple explanations of how to interpret statistics from newspapers, businesses and governments—one of my favourites is "How to Lie with Statistics" by Darrell Huff, holding up perfectly since 1954.

A more recent book, "Numbers Rule Your World" by Kaiser Fung, applies statistical thinking to a number of awesome topics — the lottery, waiting lines, and standardized tests among them. Fung's professional work is fantastic and very accessible; the book is self-recommending.

Eliezer Yudkowsky provides a highly recommended "Intuitive Explanation of Bayes' Theorem," among endless other Bayes-related posts and comments, at his eponymous website Yudkowsky.net.

Ben Goldacre's "Bad Science" work is all about how to avoid quackery in medicine — only some of the book is about statistics, but all of the book is excellent. His newspaper columns are always enjoyable and his blog, BadScience.net, is addictive reading and covers a lot of statistical topics.

Andrew Gelman's "Statistical Modeling, Causal Inference, and Social Science" blog (yes—real statisticians name their blogs like that), also known as AndrewGelman.com, generally covers more technical topics but regularly includes fantastic casual statistics anecdotes, a must-read for the true stats-addict

SOURCES

i. VARIAN: Quoted in "For Today's Graduate, Just One Word: Statistics" by Steve Lohr. New York Times, August 5th 2009. <http://www.nytimes.com/2009/08/06/technology/06stats>

ii. TRUMAN: See, for example, the "1948 United States presidential election" Wikipedia page.

iii. CENSUS: See, for example, "2010 Census" by the U.S. Government Accountability Office for both a discussion of the problem and the Bureau's attempts to fix it. <http://www.gao.gov/products/GAO-08-1167T>

Googling "census undercount" for any major city or country will almost certainly give a range of articles about undercount issues in recent censuses.

iv. ZUCKERBERG: Ok, I admit it: the actual source for this information is the movie The Social Network. But see also the "Mark Zuckerberg" Wikipedia page.

v. POLIO: See, for example, "For Today's Graduate, Just One Word: Statistics" by Steve Lohr. New York Times, August 5th 2009. <http://www.nytimes.com/2009/08/06/technology/06stats>

vi. WOLFERS: from "What Drives Obesity?" by Justin Wolfers. Freakonomics.com, June 16th 2011. <http://www.freakonomics.com/2011/06/16/what-drives-obesity-an-economist-takedown-of-the-economist/>

vii. HOLMES: From "The Sign of the Four," by Sir Arthur Conan Doyle.

viii. RUTHERFORD: A truly engaging history of the development of physics in the 20th Century — why successive theories, including

Rutherford's, came to be accepted and then in turn surpassed — can be found in John C. Polkinghorne's "Quantum Theory: A Very Short Introduction." Available on Amazon, etc. Any number of examples from that book, such as the rise of Einstein's Theory of Relativity, illustrate the same point about Bayesian reasoning. A good description of the Geiger-Marsden experiment can be found on its Wikipedia page.

ix. DOCTORS: See, for example, "Interpretation by Physicians of Clinical Laboratory Results," by Casscells, Schoenberger and Graboys, New England Journal of Medicine 1978, 299:999-1001.

x. CLARK: For a fuller discussion of the Sally Clark trial, see Ben Goldacre's book "Bad Science." Available on Amazon, etc. Relevant coverage is also given on the "Sally Clark" Wikipedia page.

xi. EINSTEIN: This quote is attributed to "Albert Einstein's teacher, 1895" in various parts of the internet, for example on the "Incorrect Predictions" Wikiquote page; however, no name is given and there is no original source, so the story may be apocryphal.

The cover image on this book is "Portrait of Felix Nadar (1820-1910), Photographer and Aeronautical Scientist," Unidentified Photographer, Prior to 1910, released to the commons by the Smithsonian Museum under the "no known copyright" attribution. If you believe that this image is copyright, please contact the publisher immediately. Cover design by the author; there isn't a clever allusion there, I just really liked the picture.

ACKNOWLEDGEMENTS

The smaller the writer, the bigger his debts.

This print edition is dedicated to Zihao Xu, without whom it never would have been finished. Zihao has taught me more than almost-anyone about how to become good at things, by his insights and by his example.

An enormous, inexpressible "thank you" goes out to all the friends who gave love, comments, belief and attention to the text of this book, and its author. I will never be able to convince you guys how much you meant, for the book and to me.

Marian Messing gave spectacular editing advice, heart-warming encouragement, and awarded this project the highly-coveted "neato" designation; I really couldn't be more grateful.

Lauge Schøler went above and beyond to become an editor on the project, and redoubled my belief that there was a point to writing this. I don't think he knows how much he helped this book come together.

Tristan Spaulding has ridiculous insight into how people think, and wasn't afraid to tell me when my writing sucked, and both of those things were rare, spectacular and indescribably helpful.

Abigail Bowman cajoled and encouraged me to finish the book after I'd hit the "I don't want to be here" plateau, as well as providing endless technical support and lots of great company. Thank you for everything.

Susanna Dunn always knows the right thing to say, and says it; I'm incredibly lucky to have her in my life.

Deborah Chang is amazing. It's impossible to describe how much better things are after getting her advice, support and encouragement.

Esther Breger suggested writing this book in an off-hand comment over a cup of coffee, triggering the longest post-coffee project I have ever attempted. Some day I hope I can repay Esther the favour.

The following people kindly agreed to read drafts and offer suggestions: Jason Yun, Derek Gideon, Michaela Shaw, Charley Jarrett, Jon Hezghia, Zihao Xu, Saraswathi Shukla, Sukrit Silas, Maddy Case, Oguzhan Atay, Katie Hsih, Malavika Balachandran, Tony Hu, Rajiv Ayyangar, Elizabeth Cooper, Kelly Lack, Shivani Radhakrishnan, Clement Canonne, Jon Giuffrida, Deepa Iyer, and Sarah Dykstra (order randomised, in the strict sense). Endless thanks to all of you for your thoughtful comments and suggestions.

The residents of New Bealand gave me home and hope when the book was just beginning, as well as a box in the corner with my name on it and my heart in it; unending gratitude to Sandra Thomas, for things that can't be said in words. Dan Yagudin and Sarah VanWagenen were both invaluable and delightful right before publication. Many others have been nice to me, fed me, and encouraged my nerdiness; this book wouldn't be here without you. Thank you.

Professor Hugo Simão taught me formal statistics, and how much professors can care about students; Professor John Londregan showed me how smart you can become if you really spend time thinking about things; Martin Schmalz and Professor Faruk Gul encouraged me with economics when I'd basically given up. Thank you to all of them for saving me academically.

Finally, I would never have written this book without the wisdom of Paul Graham, who changed the way I think about work. In the age of the Kindle, the only obstacles to getting published are the bad habits that stop us making things other people want. If you'd like to write a book, write one. I'm looking forward to reading it.

1199324R00029

Made in the USA
San Bernardino, CA
29 November 2012